Aging Towards My Freedom

A Collection of Poems

Samuel Mann

Self Publisher

Contents

Foreword

Why settle for such a weird title, Aging towards my freedom? After all, some curious young readers might be tempted to ask what does growing old has to do with one's freedom? And my initial response would then be something like this: many of us naturally seek to become independent as we approach adulthood. When we are born we are born free only to have our freedom constricted during our childhood and teenage years. The French existentialist philosopher Jean Paul Sartre believed that man is condemned by his freedom. In other words, for Sartre freedom is with us everywhere for the duration of our lives and whatever we do is a result of that unconscious ability to choose. Yet, unfortunately, in most cases that ability to choose is conditioned by a rational imperative to conform to prescribed expectations or societal norms which Freud earlier described in psychoanalytical terms as a struggle between the Id and the Ego. Now I'm afraid I am appearing to contradict myself if according to Sartre our freedom is always with us, notwithstanding the choices we make. To be or not to be, that is how the reverent English playwright William Shakespeare interpreted it at ground zero level. The difference, however, between Sartre and my own concept of freedom is that he was circumstantially looking at it as a pre-existential option whereas I prefer to see it as an unwinding process of self rediscovery, a take back movement to regain at least some of the freedom we lose in our acquiescence to follow the rules of society.

Having said so, I now am obligated to translate what I mean by this in more realistic jargon. To do so you'll forgive me if I have to backtrack a little in time. Several years ago a certain friend on social media whose name I cannot divulge confided in me that she was being uncomfortably seduced by an old married friend. Being the naïve gentleman I was, I innocently told her that in my observation older men tend to be inclined towards taking more liberties for themselves which to their delight conveniently encompasses the opposite sex as well. At the time I was growing passionately involved with poetry so much so that her intimation gave rise to the idea for a poem which I entitled, Aging towards my Freedom. Today when I look back over the years and where I am at present I realize that I have crossed the Rubicon of my youth and that I can no longer deny my tenuous situation between middle age and that creeping threat of seniority. All throughout my younger days I had championed William Wordsworth's Intimation of Immortality like a youth who was literally ahead of his age, "What though the radiance which was once so bright be now forever taken from our sight, We will grieve not but find strength in what remains behind." But this is not what the collection of poems in this book is about. I am not reminiscing nostalgically about the past. Rather, it's the opposite: I am welcoming the freedom that comes with growing older.

Paradoxically, it is the baby boomers who once protested the war in Vietnam and came together in the name of peace and love at Woodstock who are now the most conservative bastions of the status quo. As a great admirer of the sixties and the fabulous music and artistes that emerged from that era it pains me to see how this generation have evolved into anti-peace, anti-freedom, anti-youth and anti-progressive reactionaries. Needless to say, how shocked I was at the generational divide in the Brexit outcome and the polling of Americans in the recent Democratic primaries. How a millennial woman was thrown under the bus for two septuagenerian candidates. In a sense, therefore, what I am writing about in my poems goes against the grain of this disheartening truth. As a baby boomer myself I am inspired and energized by millenials and genzees taking ownership of their future. We need to simply back off and allow the youths to take over.

Even though I may look old in appearance my mind is still young and has not aged a day. Could this be the reason why I am still so passionate about freedom, injustice, literature and politics?

The poems in this collection are divided into four categories: Aging and Freedom, Art and Love, Eros and Acts of Defiance. My emphasis though is on the first category because it is the theme that is interwoven throughout the book. For me, aging is like dying and like dying, as Sylvia Plath wrote, it is an art and an art which only becomes more subtle professionally with each passing day. In my case, being a visual artist also I see it as a canvas of surrealism filled with all the sparkling elements of eccentricities, fleeting reflections, outlandish freedom and behaviour, idealism, openness, humanitarianism, empathy, love, equality, justice, pain, bitterness and sadness. The other categories are more specific and focused in messaging. I think it is obvious that I am influenced a lot in my poems by the visual arts and writers such as Charles Bukowski, T.S. Eliot and perhaps most of all the post modernist philosophy of Jean Baudrillard whose poetic reflections of a dystopian reality has helped me to amplify and open up my own perception of life.

Part One: Aging with Freedom

"I grow old ... I grow old ...
I shall wear the bottoms of my trousers rolled."

~T.S. Eliot, The Love Song of Alfred J. Prufrock

"Man is condemned to be free; because once thrown into the world, he is responsible for everything he does."

~ Jean Paul Sartre

Aging Towards My Freedom

I say to hell with hopes
Let's grab the reins of our dreams
And unchain the feelings we nurtured for so long.

The volatility of friendly conversations
Forces me to make Freudian slippages just like that
Re-opening old crushes like earthquakes
And preceding my reputation with volcanic ashes.

An exile in the darkness of my own incarceration
Susceptible lately to the nuances of the environment
I score dozens of karma points attending
to lost kittens
Meowing in the hallways of tenement buildings.

Famished by the hunt for new beacons of inspiration
I re-interpret the world to rescue an illusion,
Scavenging every corner of the planet
Before grandly announcing my renewed arrival.

Apologies Regretted

A world without bombs,
Without the fear of foreigners
Presuming to take over their countries,
Their jobs, their women, their culture,
Without the superficiality of apologies,
Insincere promises of we can and we will.
People who think for themselves
and people who let others think for them.

Virtual reality at its best
In an Age of the New Normal
Where distancing and hiding behind a mask
Constitute the preferred mystery of romance.
The ladies burn themselves at the stake
Like modern Jeanne D'Arcs but only much older,
Martyrs regretting and refusing to apologize
But rising up poetically from their ashes.
People who believe in forgiveness
And people who don't forgive.

Things we see when we're young
And things we don't anymore, because we're older,
Snowflake boomers using respect to roadblock
Millennial fighting to make this world a better place
And all others daring to challenge their illusions,
The aesthetics of appearance
That can only fictitiously express itself
In lateral languages of a certain kind.
People who think outside the box
and people who're afraid of leaving their boxes.

Contributions of Insanity

The immorally unscrupulous,
Playfully and provocatively wicked,
A global cast of featured artists,
Sensuously and uproariously funny,
An unfinished work of art
Painted with the richness of sins,

The biblical tree of evil,
Embellished with the diversity of autumn,
A harem of love, lust and forgiveness,
You will find among us
Women and men of loose characters
Parading audaciously down a mad catwalk.

The not too right in the head,
Obsessive compulsive disorders,
Flirt addicts, bitches and goddesses,
Cougars, tiggers or players,
The fraped and the abused,

Pillow wrestlers who laundry at nights.
The lonely and heart-broken,
Divorcees, insomniacs, romanticists,
Mystery, narcissism and sarcasm,
Scoops of interlectual (sic) dialogues,
Aspiring artists, poets and story tellers
Singing and dancing in a theatre of laughter.

Conversations from the gutter,
Blow up dolls, sex maniacs and constant travelers
This and so much more...all wrapped up,
All rolled into one huge silvery cloud
Fading and vanishing into my passion
To reincarnate the history of romance.

A Don Juan with his ship of flowers
Sailing across the turbulent sea of words
Carrying a secret chest of poems
Dedicated to the goddess of apathy,
My contribution to insanity
Where repetition is the science of love.

Guilty

Everyone has his apocalypse;

Mine is the hurdle every morning of jumping
out of bed,

Shielding my eyes from the first rays of sunlight,

Tightly pulling the pillow across my face

And wrapping it around my head

To suppress the pain of awakening.

I'm asphyxiated by the dawn of a new normal

Threatening me like a pandemic everywhere I turn

In the years that bring the philosophic
whiteness to my hair.

Descending gracefully from the clouds

I inebriate myself with pages of knowledge

To spew my wisdom upon a world
disappearing from itself.

Guy Debord's Society of the Spectacle,

So risk averse to the point of tragi-comedy,

Mass surveilling one another with mistrust,

Taping our physical boundaries
with arrows and circles

To avoid any danger of potentially uniting,

Playing the game of cops and robbers
with our neighbours,

And kneeling religiously upon their throats

To hear them cry, "I can't breathe!"

Guilty for all the wrong reasons

Says the media, handing down its verdict,

Victim shaming the poor and vulnerable

For experiencing the pain of discontent,

Just to re-enforce the privileges of the one percent.

A rebel against the culture of fear,

I'm angry that my silence is rudely misconstrued

By someone in a café

Whose injured leg is resting on a chair next to me

While I look the other way,

Coerced to hide my face from the
chaos about to unfold,

At the long gone dream of affluence

Drowning out by the mighty roar of
millennials and genzees

Marching and daring to create a brave

new world of their own!

The Man who pretended to be a Goat

Out of the POT he was,

High on grass,

Ven this man Ric-ocheted like a Rock

Off to a mountain.

Some say it was the curried goat that got to him

But others believed, no,

He must've been bewitched

By the Cynthia-lating pepper pot he ate

That Persaud-ed him to become a goat,

Austin-tatiously surviving Alan

As he Mann-fully roamed the hills and forests.

O-Kay, Leight(er)on, Diane but en-
Joy-ing his life to the fullest

Though Susan, his wife, Denice

He was ever a happily married man.

The Birthing of the Older Man Inside

Smile though you're growing older,
Smile though the world is getting colder,
Smile though you need a shoulder,
Smile for soon it will all be over.

Don't you just hate birthdays
That only make you wish you were young again.
The years eat you like the cake they serve.
With one swoosh they snuff you out,
Leaving only the darkness for you to reflect upon.

The voices you can hardly hear
Echoing around your ears
A familiar song so often played before.
Without listening you know it like
the sound of silence .

Even the wine is younger than you

And what's worse it even tastes better

But you have no other choice than to swallow
your pride

And drink it anyway

For in spite of all the philosophic yearnings
and ART-ifice

The meaning of life still eludes you.

Hope

Silhouetted by towering trees
An island where dreams melt like butter
And pride, screaming in defiance,
Plunges through an open window,
Where the past is everything and nothing,
Where the future is upside down
And vague memories are all that's left behind.

My head is too light
For the icy winds weighing into my ears
And rifling through my collar,
Pounding the hard paves
With a pair of worn out leather shoes
I am tenderized by my weary feet.

The gory impression of an artist
Trampled upon by the monstrosity
He created out of temptation,
What seems normal to him

But to the red headed lady not,

Enthroned on her pedestal rim,

Tossing a silver insignia into the air,

To question whether the truth is cast

In black and white?

Whether what is right is wrong,

Good is bad or vice versa?

Every inch of the way,

Be it men or women,

Great thinkers keep shifting the goal post

Blinded by the need to see both sides,

And turning everything into faceless abstractions

Like an old professor and his unfinished book,

Adrift in the mercurial tides of change,

Never sure if he has penned his last sentence.

The Dream Reader

Dreams of dream do I read
Chosen by us not but of someone else
Whose why's are multiple choices in a test
Rightly filled with the wrong answers.
Tell me, what is it you dream
And stories will I tell of lives larger
Than heroes or heroines?
A man and a child,
A boyfriend and a lover,
Deep canals moving along dark lonely streets,
Self driven cars
To a country house where rests a tiger in its garage,
Firewalled outside a garden of roses and lilies
To keep intruders out,
Hungry for fishes as the lady of spring
Sits and sips on her bench
Pots of coffee served by a posthumous artist
Who sadly lost his ear at a wishing well.
The card I flip at the end

Between my fingers

No one understands.

Life is but a gamble I repeat,

Played at intervals between sleep and wake

Neither side apologizing

Nor compromising with even a single handshake.

I have this great big fantasy

I have this great big fantasy
Where artists rule the world
And their subjects happily dwell in portraits
As unicorns roam the landscape.

I have this amazing dream
In which beautiful women
Turn wicked men into princes
And good men into frogs
With a mere glance from their magic eyes.

I have this giant bubble
Growing inside my head;
One day I fear it's going to pop
And then I'll wake up wondering
If I've become the new Rip Van Winkle.

I have this strange notion
That I've been hiding all the time
Inside the pages of a dictionary

Whose meanings are empty
And every word is written backwards.

I have this numb feeling in my feet
The bottom under me is caving anytime
To welcome my soul with outstretched arms
Into its towering abyss of the damned.

I have this D-day blast
Watching myself implode
Like an old demolished building
Subsiding fatally into the ruins of my ashes.

Felicity the Mysterious Cat

The gray cat is on the prowl again
Scouring for his next victim to begin,
Another night she'll never forget
After he's made her thoroughly wet,
Hypnotizing her with his diamond shaped eyes
While his shadow dances to her cries
Silhouetted against a smoke fest wall
Like a secret trophy doll.

The perverted rays of sunlight
Creeping through an open window
Unmask a pair of porcelain thighs to his sight
Slipping out from under the covers below.

It's happy hour at the bar
And everyone is singing like a star.
Drinks are on the house
And I'm contemplating if I should espouse
The red headed lady sitting with a cigarette
in her corner,

If she could teach me, a naïve learner,
The things I was never taught before.

Fatigued at his beguiling romance,
Felicity the mysterious cat
Decides she'll never take another chance
Except to remain behind her charm
And avoid his despicable chat.

I Live in a House with Glass Roof

When the hurricanes came I was afraid
All the houses in my town would lay scattered
But mine alone survived the tirade.
Either because I had remained aloof
Or that I never allowed my faith to be altered,
Aware that I was living in a house with glass roof.

Last night I slept with a lion
Though many times afraid I would be bitten,
Feeling his jaws rubbing up against my neck
As if my time alive had come to be eaten.
Something inside to me did caution
Never forget to keep a wild animal in check.

Emptying myself each day,
I struggle to keep my head above water.
Knowing I'm only a few steps away from the edge

Makes me desperate to become an author

With so much remaining I need to say,

All my secret promises just waiting
for someone to pledge.

Forgetting God was not what I had in mind.

You know I'm not the kind of man who prays.

Somewhere along the trip we accidentally
drifted apart

With me being carried away by the chase

And leaving the bonuses and the trifles behind.

Now that the end is nigh together a
new path we must chart.

On Being Short

How could you
Not see me
Standing so tall before your eyes
Like the CN tower
Overlooking the skyline
Of your cursive architecture?

I used to think
Being short was a psychological thing,
The reason why Judy Garland
Overdosed herself in her room;
Why Napoleon decided to change the world.

But when I saw
Mickey Rooney and Danny De Vito
Substituting the pride
I never felt before
And renewing my hopes in humanity
I knew I was wrong.

I smiled,

Gladly listening, as I sat

Next to my Caribbean neighbour

Advocating and championing

To an international community

The virtuosity of size

How small is beautiful

With nano technology

On the forefront of science

And terabytes of data compressed

Into tiny chips

I feel I'm the missing link

To a technological future.

In developed societies

Smaller homes are engineered

To create more space

To enlarge the privacy of our minds

Than to measure

The poverty of our material possessions.

How could you

Not see me

Costumed in my gray flannel suit

Wearing a black tie
To elevate you up into the sky
Where there's a place
We don't know yet how far it lies,
A gallery of time where
Sculpturing is an art
We use to perfect ourselves,
And from inside our hearts
We orchestrate symphonies
To accompany us on our journey.

Men with Glasses

Men with glasses
Looking adorably sexy and astute
Distinguished by the obscurity of their faces
Among a company of women who are cute.

Men with glasses
Known for the stealthy nature of their professions
Leaving behind no sign of traces
Except for their trademark of overt operations

Men with glasses
Wearing head bands and baring their chests
Tapping away at drums in private lounges
Where exotic women move like ladies
brimming with zests

Men with glasses
Talking to themselves, passionate but not insane
Listening to the orgy of female voices
Repeatedly chanting aloud their mantras in the rain

Men with glasses
Devoutly staring at open windows
Abstaining from the intrigue of sexual passes
And earnestly believing they could fly like sparrows

Moment of Truth

A self fulfilling prophesy,
The moment of truth
Unfurling like a smoke ring,
Reluctant in anticipation.
Submerged into the river of my fear,
I am no superman
Wearing a flying cape
Or a diving angel
Plunging out of a gaping sky
Listening to the chiming of a quaint old clock
Telling me it is time.
They say a wounded animal jumps highest
To exhale its last breath;
Some call it, 'tough love'
Rubbing my back
With the coldness of their hands.
Children playfully close their eyes and purse their lips
Aiming to blow my dandelion parachutes away.
Bared to my last fabric of civilization

About to turn a new leaf in the dark secrets of life,

Whoever said time enjoyed is time not regretted?

What was I hoping to find?

Digging deeper and deeper

Into the archaeology of my soul

As if desperate to unearth the ancestral homo erectus.

I've flirted, I've loved, I've laughed,

Endured the ordeal of my deception

And in the end confessing,

Only to be surprised at my innocence

Strengthened in weakness yet rejoicing

The blackest hour is closest to my newest day!

Tip toeing on the edges of reality

Together, you and I,
We had crossed the finishing line,
Without knowing but denying the present
And laughing at the future.

Chewing avocadoes and musing
Over tea as we tip toed along the edges of reality
Mesmerized in the dark
By the glow of our own shadows.

Our icy feet covered in woolly socks
beneath the electric blanket and
Wearing thick jumpers and fleecy throw overs
We procrastinate before the oncoming changes.

Knowingly we smiled at each other,
Studying the mirrored reflection of two naked bodies

Trapped inside a crystal canvass,
Wondering how did we ever lose control?

In the ephemeral glory of the final moment
We gracefully hot tub together
Sharing a glass of wine while watching ourselves
Slowly disappear into the morrow of farewell kisses.

My Dream of a Michelangelo

Come let me share with you
My dream of a Michelangelo,
The intellectual artist chiselling away
With his wit and humour, pen in one hand
Brush in another, the drapes of a nubile society
Deflowered by dirty greedy old men.

Quarantined in my forested isolation
I flirt with the truth, making passes at every woman,
The scoundrel of an artificial utopia I'm blacklisted,
Unfriended and deleted by those who are offended,
Re-vitalized by the nostalgia of sentimental songs
Or the drama of lovers in a romantic comedy,

Deteriorating with every second
Tick tock tick tock... I hurl upon the world
The obscenities of my existential quest
To re-conquer a freedom that was stolen from us,
Crafting the art of my prophetic mission

Before a crowd of indifferent pedestrians.

Sometimes the clown, sometimes the philosopher

But most times a dreamer and a stalker,

Deviously marching behind a loose
band of dissidents,

Radical protégés of the infamous Goodman era,

Avid fanatics of the Beatles, Dylan
and the Rolling Stones

Bewitched and dying to invoke the
magic of a lost Sixties.

The creation of a plasma phenomenon

Carbon copied from the structure of a DNA

And layered with the seven levels of energy,

I redefine and rewrite man made boundaries,

A post modern re-incarnation of Simon de Bolivar

Liberating the lost and the depressed

With howls of 'What the FUCK is wrong with you?'

Rope Walking Across the Niagara

Rope walking across the Niagara,
Pushing the boundaries to their extremes,
A coin spinning on its rim
Without being afraid to lose its balance,
What's the use of talking?
People only listen to all the good things I say,
The bad ones they always hear,
We know the difference,
Any fool for that matter.
From now on I will close my mouth
Like a book that has never been opened,
Is it because I've already been sold,
Read and put away forever?
Others carry bookmarks with them
To be returned to at a later date.
Mine is still to be read.
I fear my author is undecided,

Not sure as to how it should end,
A sequel perhaps?
Until every reader is tired of me
You and I will never know,
As long as the last page
Remains an unfinished task,
Pass me a cigarette, you idiot!
I can feel the nightmares coming again.
Sleeping beauty was no favourite of mine

Not feeling alright

Shadows drip
From a fractured sky,
Morphing into congregations
Of old women
Clutching at black umbrellas;
Meanwhile, pools of reflection
Mirror the shiny surfaces
Of playful vanity
Strolling with two pocketed hands
Buried inside a pair of colourful jeans;
Dragons unfurl from the clouds
To wing their escapade
Into my surrealist world;
Too weak to continue
This solemn journey of religion
I pause to un-wash my desperate soul
With the pleasures of a human holograph,
Redecorating my walls with pungent kisses
And worshipping instead

The uplifted heels of young sirens.

Outside I have no one to tempt me

Out of my loneliness,

As each is bowed before her tiny screen,

Texting prayers to a beloved one.

Hiding between cracks of lines,

I secretly apologize

For mistakes that have never been made

And through my crumpled art

And musings of wild philosophic yearnings

Strive to rid the world of my incurable madness.

In no mood to be arsed

Shall I hide my latest drawing
The one with the bare naked lady
And her back and bottom facing us?
You said you were in no mood to be arsed
So I guess I have to be careful,
Watch my words
And avoid the use of ifs and buts
In sentences and conversations
Likely to be skewed
Or digressed into topics that can lead to nowhere
When I am speaking to my friend,
Speculating about history and the West,
About gunfighters and bandits
Trapped at the tail end of a bungled attempt
To rob a bank,
About dreams that leave us wondering
What might have been,
And misinterpreting the metaphors
We see in our sleep.

Shall I cover my drawing again, dear,
The one with the bare naked lady
And her back to us?

Source Code

I wear a patch over one eye
And a ring in my left ear
To source my way into the future.
They say I hijack programs of the mind
And pilfer treasures of the heart,
That destiny is a random affair.
But with my Excalibur sword
I charge into the frequencies of time
And hack away at events
To coincide with the perfidy of my crime.

Those who cannot see me
Shall feel the trembling impulses of my voice
Echoing throughout their sleepless nights.
They that do kneel before the drums
of my thunderous strides,
Offering to welcome me
With toasts of wine pouring from their lips
And volumes of French kisses

To quench my insatiable appetite.

At nights the women roll out their bodies

To cushion my cantankerous head

With the bubbly pillows of succulent breasts

And shrink wrapping me with the smoothness

Of their flesh...

The Spot

At this spot before many times
I stood and turned around
Without counting the dusted shelves of memories,
Procrastinating among uncertainties of hope.
This time it was different:
My life never looked back.
One word, a phrase or line,
Enough how suddenly
Vanished all
In the rising flames of tomorrow.
No one saw a thing,
Not even the ashes,
The disappointment I was prepping myself for
Fled like the fluttering fingers of the wind,
Skating over the placid ocean that
was too deep in thought
To feel the friction of several aborted farewells,
Conversations we anticipated
That were almost but never spoken

Through sealed lips smiling at each other,
Projecting the negative celluloid of history
Inside a transparent frame of mind
As if to reconstruct would recreate
The 'ifs' and 'buts' into particles of yes,
Cutting away swiftly to the chase,
To sacrifice unfinished businesses
Filled with deflated desires and hunger,
And losing the goal eventually out of pure fatigue
In the long awaited sobriety of adulthood.

The Python Pursuer

Swinging from a pendulum
The answer to my quest;
Someone kneeling in a church
Praying to be strong,
Taking an oath of silence
To entomb a corporeal sin.
The tarot reader is confused
At the strange layout of her cards;
An old fortune teller gazes
Perplexedly at her clouded crystal ball.
The python pursuer is swallowed up
by his chase.
A lonely woman
Discards her feelings
And sets out for a romantic weekend
Somewhere far
Somewhere where no one will ever find her,
Searching for dragons and unicorns
Instead of heroes

Among the country sides
Where a crazy middle-aged man,
Coughing up his lungs
And giving up any hope of sleep
To be digested in the belly of a mid-life crisis,
Turning on the TV
Discovers there's nothing else
Besides an old Kirk Douglas movie
Filmed sometime back in the 1940's,
Where a jealous husband at the end
Shoots his wife and himself,
Un-answering the question: why?

The Passenger

Sitting idly by and staring
At the cluster of grumpy faces
A crowd of weary passengers
Sporting worried looks on the worm-like train
Some pretending to be absorbed in spidery lines
Of silly paperback novels,
Others flipping pages of newspapers
As if to say, 'we're all busy;'
A few filling out empty slots of crossword puzzles
Knowing they will never be completed.
A couple seats away
The pretty Eastern European woman
Is shooting straight through me
With thoughtful eyes
And crossing a pair of lovely thighs
As though nothing in the world
To her will matter anymore;
Standing next to me
And peering over my shoulders,

A semi bald Arab
With his Hercule Poirot moustache
Studies on his feet
A flat pair of shiny triangular shoes
Whose leathery odour rises up
Like hungry pigeons circling
Over my crumby head.
Opposite me the old Negro lady
Wearing a colourful head tie
Clutches her chequered handbag
And squints behind a pair of thick old fashioned rims
As if unsure of where the next stop will be.

The Simulacrum of the List

The list is long
And rambles on
Like a highway full of names,
Apocalyptically walking
From continent to continent,
Twisting and turning,
Straight and crooked,
Making U-turns at the wrong direction,
Spanning epochs of the 60's, 70's and 80's,
A mosaic of all colors:
Black, brown, yellow, pink and white.
Stamped with the faces of every kind:
The beautiful and not so beautiful,
The poor and hungry and not so poor and hungry,
Some as nice as the Norwegian soprano, Sissel,
and some not as nice,
Some young and some not as young anymore,
Artists, poets, musicians, dancers,
singers, comedians,

Unrequited lovers with Troubadours in waiting

Who line the streets at every corner.

Each step along the way

A moment to savour and treasure

With the sweet smell of coffee

Percolating through the air.

In the mornings, in the afternoons

And at evenings effeminate shapes of burgundy wine

to sip slowly from their mouths,

Here and there a kiss across the cheeks,

Accidentally grazing the lips

And leaving their faces in clouds of doubts.

Does it have a heart this all inclusive garden
of strangers?

But, of course, you wonder

For even the Devil and his advocates

are welcome at the gates of heaven,

Greeted and forgiven with a smile

Worshipfully hailed, "You are the list!"

Instead of the cold silences of revenge

And so the list continues…

The simulacrum of names and numbers,

Shopping as each is consumed by
the bucket of their totality

Neither wishing for what else is left
but the surfeit of dreams,

Surrendering our specificity

To someone whose omnipresence

is the symbol of all men

And to whom any of them is worthy of him!

Waiting

I hear the lonely cry of a baby,
The clattering footsteps of restless children,
Adults waiting for their flu shots
Or to be treated for an illness of some kind.
It's already half past
The hour of the doctor's appointment
And I'm wondering why
I'm still here,
Shipwrecked
Like Robinson Crusoe
Among a strange orientation of people.
They make you wait
As if waiting is all you do in life.
The Filipino receptionist at the counter
Smiles as she announces with an accent
The name of someone sitting in a corner
The lady next to me asks
What am I thinking?
She notices I haven't said a word

Since we came in together.
She doesn't know
I'm thinking how to say
What I want to say,
How to poeticize this environment
To make it say what I want to say
And why I feel like quitting.
She doesn't know
I'm tired watching the news on TV,
Tired of all the lies and propaganda
They keep feeding us everyday,
How we're standing at the edge of a fiscal cliff,
How many more people will be laid off
Instead of getting laid.
Austerity is revered as a miracle cure
For the sins of the world
While the income inequality gap widens
And global warming is perennially ignored,
Security reinforced with fear,
Wars waged to enrich the few.
Last night I saw a documentary
On the man who invented modern art
And when I looked at the pictures

Hanging on my wall
I realized the people in it were dead.
They had nothing to tell me.
They were bored just like me.
We were tired of each other.
Who gives a rat's ass what some bourgeois artist
Painted two centuries ago?
What does he know about the modern world?
Artists only paint themselves into a corner
Out of pure unavoidable ignorance.
Happiness is a financial bubble
Spiking and crashing
When the speculator has had enough.
I'm afraid to drink
For fear it will only worsen my sadness,
Cause me to do something stupid
Like smashing the screen of my computer
Or slamming the keyboard with my fists.
Where is Sartre when you need him?
Albert Camus or Franz Fanon?
No matter how hard I try to concentrate
My hand would not go away.
It keeps reminding me I belong to it

And I could never escape my body,
Could never alienate myself
From the wall of people encasing me.
I could never negate the white man's world.
I was trained to forget my culture and my past.
Mirrors lied to me every time I searched.
People think I'm biased and tunnel vision
But I see no desperate flare ahead of me.
I'm not even eccentric, I'm only awkward
That's all
I imagined inspiration could be measured
Against love
Only to be frustrated at my failed attempts
each time,
Accentuating my own jealousy beyond recovery.
Finally the receptionist calls her name
And we stood up
'Room six,' she says.
For a moment it sounded like sex
But that was just my twisted voice
Intervening uninvited.
I'm hopeless alas.
That's what happens

When you can't tell the difference
Between pornography and art.
Why would a group of women
Want to admire other women?
Beats the hell out of me
But that's another story...

Kaleidoscope

What if you knew me
If you didn't?
What if you wish you hadn't?
A kaleidoscope of flowers
Revolving with colourful memories.

Wired to my emotions,
I question the existence of God;
Debating the wisdom of providence
In a world without reality;
Seeking only perfection among the chaos.

Fashioning my options
Like a designer
Pole dancing with the grace of a ballerina
Whose aim is to cloak
The barrenness of his ego.

A sacrifice to science
Only waiting for the dust to settle

Before talking about the future
And losing my perspective of today
To sermonize the purpose of the truth.

I am my own soul mate,
Twinned to the bride of my reflection,
Furtively celebrating and shouting
Behind a rainbow of passion
The ecstasy of our honeymoon!

Despicable Me

Who dresses like Mussolini,
Colors himself like Idi Amin,
Wears a semi-moustache like Hitler,
Posts stupid things like a girl snorting
The white line on a highway,
Defends the neo-liberalist EU
And says nasty words to those
Who dare oppose his views,
Whose bantering is so absurd
It's a waste of time to listen or read,
Who doesn't belong to any group
Unless he's the one who leads,
Known as the Joker on social media,
A man who photoshops his way to fame,
Hiding in the characters of others,
Replacing the eyes of friends
And morphing their faces in halves,
Where else in the world will you find
A more despicable man

Than the one articulating these words?

Losing the Butterfly Touch

Everyone is looking at me
Thinking I will set them free
But who am I to deserve this honour
When all I am is just a silly actor?

Other guys show off their cars
While at nights I sit and drink at bars,
Going home late with poise
To have some fun with all my Barbie toys.

I wear several layers of faces
Like an onion hiding below the surfaces,
Waking up at the crack of dawn
And wondering who next will be my pawn.

Losing the butterfly touch
For me is not asking too much
So long as my trajectory
Finds its target and the payload is my story.

Not many will say I'm stylish,
Others even accuse me of being freakish,
But what does it matter?
In the end I know I'll always get my chatter.

Vulgar Man

Hey Mister! Yes you!
Scribbling lewd comments every day,
Showing inappropriate pictures
Of semi-nude women
And laughing to yourself,
Thinking others are amused.

Shame on you Mister!
Abusing art with optical illusions
Conjured up to seduce,
Simulating only lust and obsession
To choke the gutters of unsuspicious minds,
Spamming daily with your unsolicited messages.

Look at you Mister!
Eloquently swearing aloud,
Wearing that stupid black cape
And pretending to be a super hero
But underneath it just another flasher

Lurking behind the bushes.
Stop it Mister!
We've had enough of your ubiquitous lies,
Stalking every pretty face
With a plethora of unfinished sketches,
Immortalizing each one
With a tale of perfect romance

Oh you vulgar man!
Too devious to be aesthetic,
Manipulating profanely the victims
Entangled within your lurid web.
Who are you? What do you want?
Tell us or get the fuck away!

What was the Question

What do you want,
Was the question?
I've tried everything I can't
Though you never give me any suggestion.

The other day we talked about your
favourite philosopher
Whose name for some reason I don't remember
But when I applied his theory
You simply got confused and became less cheery.

So now tell me what is it you want to hear?
Is it something that should remain a secret
Or anything I shouldn't care?
Just let me know if I need to be more explicit.

That would be telling, you say.
I'd rather not be on display.
Just because he's not a woman
Doesn't mean he's insensitive to everyone.

Oh dear me I almost forgot:

Said you were a problem solver from way back when

I know, but your answers always
seem to miss the jackpot.

I'm sorry ma'm, but what was your question again?

Apodyopsis – The Story of Divine Madness

More, more egotistic and blacker
They say, than any God you can imagine;
Angels shudder at my deep bellowing voice;
The devil is excited whenever he sees me;
I make witches and bitches chant with tears,
Hobbling around giant mushrooms of fears.

Gorgeous women rip their hearts out in pieces
Just to cheer the hapless victims of my lust
Wasted lying on the sidewalks;
Nowhere in the universe is there
a spell more charming
Than the spiralling pupils of my cracked eye balls;
I can enchant entire legions of devout women
To reveal their untouched breasts and unshackled
The wildest demons imprisoned by their chastity.

So there's a lot of coffee in Brazil I hear

But beers hmm? That Icelandic volcano
again blowing its ashes

Far and wide....And who is this Anglo-Saxon

Arriving unannounced, pinting (sic) threateningly

With his sword at thee and proclaiming loudly

As he swears to the Gods his undying love of beer?

How much bitter more can one become

When there's enough bitterness in the world already?

Fading away as the two of us are having dinner

At one of the most exquisite macabre restaurants

And seated around our table the ever
thirsty Count Dracula,

The Fuhrer, Jack the Ripper and Stalin himself;

All of them our honoured guests
and celebrities of the past.

What a magnificent diversity of culture
and characters!

Is that blood or wine being served
by the nervous waiters?

Oh here comes the first course specially
concocted for us

By the most famous chefs of the world!

Faints at the sight of what seems to be a 'schädel'

Did he have too much blood to drink or what?

I'd say he's losing the plot as usual

Though no one has ever told him so as yet.

Excuse moi, but where am I and
what century are we in?

Ah yes...I almost forgot 'tis the time of romance,

Chivalry, windmills, giants, dragons, damsels
and knights,

Princes and princesses...The innocent
Belle and Milady,

Both rescued by the brave Knight of the Rose

From a disreputable band of fearsome brigands.

A virtual wedding hastily arranged

Between the princess and the illustrious Knight

As a fitting reward to the aging lover;

Together the newly couple retreats to a secret island

Called... the Place without a Name,
alias the Garden of Eden,

Enjoying an idyllic honeymoon without
need for dress or cabin;

As the days drift by the betrothed
lovers wrap themselves

Tightly in the arms of each other, feverishly
exploring together

The curve of every hill, of every tree and every wave

Rolling out from the ocean of their deepest emotion.

Sighs and stops for a moment to reflect:
'Is this the end of the story? Or Should I go on?
Haven't I sinned enough already?
Sinned beyond redemption?'
Feels a throbbing pain in the left side of his head
As his computer suddenly shuts down
and refuses to turn on;
Pushes the power button repeatedly
but nothing happens;
Finally he concedes to himself, 'I get it,
I'm paying for my sins already!'

Droops forward, squeezing his head
Like Al Pacino in Dog Day afternoon,
And wailing, 'Oh what have I done?
Encouraging my wicked thoughts to roam
Into such a disgusting city as Babylon!'
Just then he's smacked on his head
by hails of chewed tobacco
Raining profusely down from a darkening sky
As he slowly rises to glance up
at a colossal white envelope
Tumbling down upon him;

'Who would've thought,' he laughs to himself,
'They watch old western movies in heaven?'

The Woman in the Big Red Hat

Big hats, small hats, tiny hats
Funny hats, weird hats, serious hats
Dainty hats, quaint hats, saint hats
Square hats, round hats, twisted hats
Red hats, yellow hats, blue hats
Cake hats, chocolate hats, strawberry hats
Of all sizes, colors and shapes many hats.

Alas! The mad hatter has been stirred.
Clad in his Easter bonnet,
Doodling away stories of the absurd,
Laughing and rolling on his carpet
At the end of each masterpiece,
Tossing away his books in pairs
For any devilish child to read who cares.

But all he sees the moment he's awake
Is a shapely woman in her late thirties

Elegantly cat walking beside a lake,
Wearing a frosted bikini and a chain of daisies,
Clinging with both hands precariously
A big red spiralling instagram hat, and
Graciously amused by a world in combat.

Absence

Craving the days to come more quickly,
Wishing time would fly much faster
So that the distance between us
Would colossally grow into a giant.

A child afraid to part with an old pair of jeans,
Defying the wishes of his mother
Who chooses to recycle his attachment
By creating a memorabilia.

A teenager dead asleep,
Indifferent to the cries of her parents.
Wake up! It's time to go to school!
Staying away because she's no match for her peers.

A junkie swarmed by his possessions,
Protesting the notion of spring cleaning.
The heart wrenching pain of losing a loved one
Bowing at the end of his final performance.

Symptoms of withdrawal from a drug addict

Ostensibly living one day to the next,

A lover but not a loser

For whom rejection is no longer an option.

Part Two: The Art of Love

"And so art is everywhere, since artifice is at the very heart of reality. And so art is dead, not only because its critical transcendence is gone, but because reality itself, entirely impregnated by an aesthetic which is inseparable from its own structure, has been confused with its own image. Reality no longer has the time to take on the appearance of reality. It no longer even surpasses fiction: it captures every dream even before it takes on the appearance of a dream."

~ Jean Baudrillard

'Tis better to have loved and lost
Than never to have loved at all."

~ Alfred Tennyson

Come Dance with Me

Come dance with me, my sweet angel

Let me take you for a magical spin
on my short bus ride,

Circling back and forth with my pen,

The best dancer of all,

At times repeating the rhythm of my thoughts

Like a chorus to your ears

Just so to make sure you're listening

While you turn your head away

And secretly smile in your heart.

I don't need tequila or rapid hand movements

To stumble and fall, play Proud Mary
to roll up on the floor

Or win a movie extra competition.

They say too much dancing can
leave a woman exposed.

Remember the lady in the red dress

Tantalizingly revealing glimpses of her ivory thighs.

Some call it Tango or whatever Latin name it is

But my thoughts move cursively across enemy lines

Over wide open spaces of snowy sheets.

His feet may take you anywhere

But a writer's hands can teleport you
to distant places unknown.

He needs no date or vacation to the seaside

For his mind is an undisturbed castle

And in it he dances forever happily
with his captive princess

Anne of a Thousand Years

Wasn't it the face of a woman
That launched a thousand ships?
That ignited a Trojan war?
I thought it was only my imagination
Until I first saw you in The Fox.

There was poetry all along with chemistry
Pouring out from every angle of your face.
You didn't have to say anything
And yet I could feel the words trembling inside me.
Your beauty created a mighty armada of artists
Ready to wage a crusade against your critics.

Thou art but Venus to the fortunate eyes.
Your silence serenades the souls of many
For any that refuses to kneel before
The divine elegance of your presence
Is either a foolish rationalist
Or one who thinks of beauty only
as a means to an end.

I would be accused of being the meanest man alive
Were I to optimize with words
The radiance of your physical phenomenon
For words would nervously become shy
At the mere thought of you
Not even a thousand Shakespeares would suffice
To describe the feelings you ingrain in others.
Even love itself is too finite to qualify.

Thou art the Mother of all Beauty!
A portrait with a mysterious sadness,
One that makes the Mona Lisa pale in comparison.
It would take all eternity to measure
The longing in your lips and eyes,
And to infiltrate the aesthetic armour of thy face.

To be able to justify such wonder
One has to be more than just a writer,
One has to be able to sing it, draw it, paint it, dance it
And play it like an actor,
Become the angler fish to melt into it
For one glance at you annihilates
my existence forever.

You devour me like the lovely Medusa,

The ideal simulacrum in a post modernist world

Philosophically exuding compassion
and deep understanding.

So much so that the English novelist,
Charlotte Bronte,

Would've had to have you in mind

When she wrote her famous novel, Jane Eyre.

Thinking of you alone is Nirvana
to my troubled mind.

Beauty Everywhere

Among friends and lovers
I saw beauty in conversations
And with my pen I carved away the marbles
To unlock from each a poem of the heart.

In the sketches of my portraits
I saw the beauty of an unfinished life,
Musicians and artists playing on sidewalks
And below all day in subways,
Lawns that remain un-mowed for weeks,
In the dark passages of time
Where men and babies moved in and out.

I saw beauty everywhere,
In every form and every movement,
Every color that twirled around
In the carousel of your eyes.
I saw beauty in everything,
In all that was visible and even the invisible

Whose hands I felt.

I saw flashes of beauty
Emerging from inside the orange ribbons of hell.

Beauty surrounded me everywhere
Like the Ancient Mariner,
Without a drop to drink,
But never surfeiting my appetite with its abundance.

The more beauty I saw
The wider became the rift
Between my sadness and happiness.
I was a picture of Dorian Gray
Mirroring the ugliness of my beauty
And every beauty that I saw
In the infrastructure of the land,
In the architecture of the mountains,
In the faces of people
I will never know or never meet,
Voluptuous women in costumes
Prancing around to the harmony of steel pans,
Beauty of all sizes, shapes and colors
Trapped inside the perspectives of my vacant eyes.

A Surrogate Poet

The seconds tick into minutes,
Creeping lazily into the late hours
As I teasingly slipped towards the days
And fittingly jog along into weeks,
Racing ahead among the months
To be soaring high into a million years.
Still the same I remain,
Plugged into my indestructible world,
Living the virtual life,
Timelessly repeating myself
With the click of a button,
Transforming the protagonist into many characters.
No woman is beyond my infinite arms,
Some say I'm almost like any of them,
A transgender of famous movie stars.
Other times, a fearless Viking
Sailing the northern seas with my warrior princess,
About to make a triumphant entrance
At an annual game of chivalrous old men.

Someone else in the twinkling of an eye,
A total stranger you've never met,
Villain or late student of philosophy,
Nutty as nothingness,
Hard to understand
Yet feeling somewhat betrayed
By the duplicity of my art.

It is what it is

I was…but not anymore.

After I celebrated the years we'd known each other
And you didn't show up;
You made excuses
that never applied to others.
Saying you didn't understand a word I spoke
Because you didn't speak a certain language.

I was…but not anymore.

After you complained to our mutual friend
And she intervened;
You kept on denying that you didn't
Yet agreeing that it was best for us
Until one day you snapped
And finally found the courage
To say so yourself.

I was…but not anymore.

After you professed your belief in changes,
That life goes on and one has to move on,
Resulting in an argument over the future of a nation;
In the end, I couldn't get you
To change your mind.

I was…but not anymore

You wanted out and I wanted in
Just as Shakespeare's Hamlet
The question, to be or not to be,
Was decided in your favour;
Intellectually I was no match
For you and your intuition.

And I was…but now I am no longer
And so it is and what it was it remains.

For Better or Worse

You were in the room
When I entered
Lying on your stomach
Asleep, half dressed
In your black laced underwear,
Impulsively inviting me
With your thick milky thighs
to place my hands against them.

Was this really happening?
I shuddered to myself,
Confused we were together
Under the same roof.
Guests perhaps?
Weary travelers for a one night stand
Enacting an old childhood nursery rhyme
To wander where shall I find
My lady's chamber?

Someone in the dark
Whose face I could not recognize
Sat closely beside you,
No doubt murmuring sweetly
Something in your ears
While his hands were busy
Unbuttoning your blouse.
The contours of a Goddess
I saw, full-bodied and descending
A flight of stairs, saliently robed in silk,
With feet of majestic orange
And heels of silence
Firmly anchored to the surface below.

She was the meanest Muse
No compliment could ever amuse,
Nor flag nor truce, reason or truth
Impress upon, let alone her ire appease,
Who, bored by the monotony of history
And cacophony of economic promises unfulfilled,
Her divine franchise cast
Without regret and by a leap of faith
Let loose a chaos of revolution

For better or worse.

The Portrait

Golden flares of snow light shimmering
Behind groovy drapes of lemon vines
Suspended from a ceiling,
Playfully encircled by smiling leaves
Twirling sideways at the corners
To tease the mystery out of an evening.
Crystal clocks below fenders
Wave sadly at the fallen hours.

Stop the foolish rambling and draw me as I am,
Where is my nose?

A heart rolling away on two wheels
Before the sunset, anxious for the New Year
To begin.
Come back Shane! Echoes a voice
From an old favourite movie of baby boomers.
Eve's apple is lying upside down on a table,
Waiting to be bitten by a stranger

Whose fate will determine the future of a world
Separated between the luscious East and West
Thousands of years before the timely travels
Of Marco Polo and Christopher Columbus.

I don't see any neck
What is this?
You haven't sketched anything
But an abstract collection
Of vines, leaves, clocks, hearts and apples
Nor do I see any connection
Except perhaps a quaint resemblance
To one of Salvador Dali's queer masterpieces

Forgive me, Madam,
but the pale marbled pedestal
Assembled like the plot of a secret tale
Proudly stands before all to ponder and wonder
The marvel of this glorious world.

I hear a poem

No it's not what you think
Or what I believe you heard;
There's neither reason nor link
That would suggest a third.

Yours alone is the voice
That touches me in the wind;
A wave of noise
That caresses my feet in the sand.

Through the beak of a feathered pen
I hear the words of a poem
Unravelling the mystery of a friend
In someone's heart aching to find a home.

With legs crossed
And a book in my hand
I was amazed at how many times I could've been lost
But for the lines you crafted to help me understand.

Pictures of you and me
Wander forever through my mind
Adding more verses daily to the poetry
You wrote and left behind.

Would it be wrong to say
In the rhythm of your thoughts I feel
The quest of that old dreamer, Don Quixote,
Laying siege to what I believe was real.

An Awkward Encounter

When our eyes meet
Without introduction
Premeditated and hungry
Confused, hesitant, quietly,
Questioning, inviting, avoiding,
Across tables, in corridors,
During formal discussions and conversations,
Aborted attempts at socializing,
Silently observing, unnoticed and expectant.
That brief but eternal one second thrill of euphoria
When the heart suddenly becomes still,
Pausing to listen its own ringing reverberations,
Eyes clouded by the cataract of misty uncertainties.
Will it be just a matter of time or never
Before the suspense is over
And restraint is a young pregnant mother
Screaming her lungs away
At the first sign of labour
While the alchemy of two strangers

Crashes into the shoreline of no return
I am hoping and hoping...
Secretly pretending to be detached from it all
In self denial of that fated course of events
Then I heard the shocking news
In a few days you would be gone
That which I had grown accustomed to
The most valued experience of my days
Shattered in a moment's notice
Not by the wrecking ball of a wishful romance
Or the twisted comedy of a Shakespearean plot
But just plain oblivious reality
Cycling through its ruthless race of change!

Souvenirs from an Awkward Encounter

I met you in my dreams again
Last night without knowing why.
Once you returned from out of nowhere
To the place where we met before
But it was only for a day to visit.

The next time I saw you
I knew it was just a dream
For I was consciously squeezing my eye lids
As hard as I could
For them to remain closed forever.

The way you swayed in your familiar
pear shaped figure,

That look in your eyes that asked
us, "Why are we here?"

I was painting a poster of Bob Marley
And listening to the music of Hot Chocolate
When you entered the room
And, by Jove, what an impression you left,

Even to this day I still cannot forget
The sweetest perfume you wore
Bending over my shoulders
While I stupidly showed you
One of my favourite sketches.

I think I'm in love

Should I confess to her
Proudly wearing my feelings
On both my arms before it's late
Or paint a portrait of my heart
And express it to her in a FedEx envelope?
Should I write a poem
That will tickle from her lips
A smile that could enchant a stone?
Make her chuckle to herself alone
And grab a chocolate chip to digest its tone.
Maybe I could try singing one of her favorite songs
Though my voice is dry and thirsts with love
Or dance to the beat of her twinkling eyes.
Do you honestly think it will work?

Nah…I doubt it, I pretty much doubt it.
For she's already a poet
Who speaks through the voice of others,
An artist who draws people to her side,

The singer who resonates within my soul

And the dancer in everyone

That glides to the harmony of nature.

Nor am I one among the majority

But another who relies on chance

And flirts adventurously with ne'er an end in sight.

I think I'm in love and it isn't hard without a doubt

To figure out who this someone is?

So tell me, what should I do?

Imperfect Lover

I will dance for you
While preparing your meals,
Sing as I do the dishes,
Be your knight in Shining Armour
Before you retire to bed.
I will soothe your weary feet with my kisses,
Shower you with words of flowers
Because your body is a poem
Heaving with the rhythm of a sonnet
And inscribed by the finest cursive letters.
I will sketch you a thousand times
Every time you tip toe out of the bathroom
Wearing nothing else but a towel around your hair.
I will put the kid back into the kids,
Restore the fun back into the housework.
A better partner in all the world you will never find;
So kind and so full of attention,
One who will always be there at your side,
To catch you whenever you fall.

I will create the most spectacular works of art,

Color your world with the sound of laughter,

Fill the gaps of your silence with smiles together.

I will dry your tears

With the warmth of my lips.

I will scrub the floor on my knees if I have to,

Do all the laundry and groceries for you.

I will serve you coffee and eggs in bed,

Romance you with the most elegant candle
lit birthdays.

I will do all this and so much more

Because there's no other work that I crave so badly,

No other company that I dream about so madly,

No other love that I would die for so gladly!

If as you say

If as you say it is true
That I trespass your mind
More often than the trillion times
I'm convicted
Of imprisoning you
In the penitentiary of my heart
It is still not enough
To appease my Cupid imagination
That eludes every margin
To be circumscribed by it.

My aspired aim is to travel beyond
The deepest recesses of your mind,
Renouncing the nothingness of my being,
To reside among the unconscious aliens
of your soul
To contemplate its cosmic rays
From the observatory of your eyes;
The air that you breathe

I inhale within you
To sustain the flames of my desire
For I'm too afraid to lose you
To the farthest galaxy of my universe.

Death of a Poet

If you ask me
Where's my next poem
Gonna come from
I'll probably say to you
I have no clue.

My muse and I
We had a fight
And the other night
She eloped on a white horse
Leaving me without my source.

Now the voices
Won't speak to me again,
Thinking it was my fault and not my pen
I should've said no
Instead of letting you go.

The old grandfather's clock
Is ticking past the hour of despair

Confirming on the wall my biggest fear
You'd never look for me
As long as you're free.

Once upon a time
You made me passionate
When I was angry with hate
A time when for nothing else I ache
And all night stayed awake.

With celestial eyes
And gushing hair you leverage
A romance that stole my heart as hostage
Reciprocating with no follow-up other than a one line
In conversations that were too benign.

Like an artist
In need of an extraction
You pulled me into action,
Numbing away the bitterness of my pain
While from me you abstain.

But now you're gone
And there are still poems to write

Look at me sipping a glass of wine
alone in the twilight

Reminiscing the music of love

As I fade quietly away into the darkness above

The Pot

So you found a pot
And I thought to myself alone
It must be our lot
For all the battles we have sown.

Together you and I
Shall continue the search
But you interrupted and asked me why
When all that's missing is a church.

What about the gold?
I retorted with a smile.
Oh you fool that's already been sold
Stop acting as though you were never told.

You're the pot and I'm the gold
The rainbow that you saw
Was the color of my hair unrolled
So there's no need for you to become an outlaw.

Somewhere out there

Somewhere out there
Lost for words
There's a poem I feel
Whose author I can't be sure
Whether it's you or me
Or anyone I know.

For he that holds the golden pen
Without justification for ends is blind
And to the rest of the world
His confusion only writes
Being all that matters and in the now alive.

I ask neither questions nor answers
Either there are none or one too many
Something that I would never understand
So what's the use of engaging
If nothing ever will I be told.
Somewhere out there
I see a poem

And it's not me or you or them
But just a poem,
One that is recited from the heart,
Blowing like dandelions in the wind
And rolling its words into little verses of cotton.

If only I knew
What this poem was about
Then I could close my eyes at last
And bid my love to you goodnight.

The Winter of My Poetry

When you fell upon me
It was the winter of my poetry.
Blizzards of words cascaded from the sky
Till I was cold and hungry
But the fire in your lips
Kept the frozen ice caps off my feelings
To usher in the summer of my love.

That night you wore a short dress
And it escalated the scorching lava
Simmering through the veins of my flesh.
I silently watched you danced your
hips across the room
Like a belly dancer swaying inside my head.
We spoke for hours late into the morning
About everything and about nothing.

The grey circles of smoke above our bed
Reminded us of planets from another universe
Vying for our unknown destination

While the soft tapping of tabla drums
And twanging of sitar strings
Lifted us gently into the lingerie of the stratosphere.
Throughout the evening your eyes became moist
From the pathos of an unhappy tale
But you kept on smiling
And even though you pretended to laugh sometimes
I could still see the glistening reflection on your face.

We had found each other at last
And it was neither love at first sight
nor any crush at all
But a few years of intellectual nurturing,
Sudden outbursts of anger, misunderstandings,
Sharing of intimate thoughts and
quiet moments together,
Being there for each other, never ignoring
or overlooking,
Never unconditional but reciprocal
and complementing.

Our rendezvous was the tipping point of our descent
Into a crater of no return,
The endgame of a calculated foreplay,
Knowing an eruption of the heart

Would be fatal to the union of two souls
Separated by the transparency of time and space.
We parted with a flurry of kisses and hugs,
Before waving goodbye to the dawn of a new day.

The Word

And there was no beginning
And there was no word
For if there were,
None of them made any sense at all
Nor did anyone hear them anyway.

And nothing was created in my name
Except the tragedy of my demise,
An earth melting like a popsicle in my hands.
And the rivers all became dry
As the Kalahari desert
For I had no more tears to shed

And there was no heaven and earth
But an effigy of my soul
Burning in the wind.
And I was angry again,
I had failed the test of creation,
Instead of life I had produced collateral damage

Instead of a brave new world
I had brought horror and destruction,
I had wasted seven days
With the seeds of my infertility.

The other Gods laughed at me,
They knew I had to be insane,
Either that or I was just another imposter.
But Eros alone was sad,
I could tell from the look in his eyes
He was disappointed.
Of all the Gods he had failed the most
And he had high hopes in me.
I felt like a gardener without a garden,
An Adam without an Eve,
My scripture was of no use to anyone,
I was a God whose humanity would never be forgiven.

Tubes of Colors

Tubes of colors
Buried inside a tinted box
Lying next to a spirited jar
And brunette brushes
All dressed up in their white uniform.

For many years
And from places to places
I carried you
And your folded easel
Like a souvenir
Reminding me of something
That once impassioned me in my youth.

At times I un-clicked the lock
Just to steal a precious glance at you,
Secretly afraid your genie
Would jump at me.
But after our long separation of divorce

My confidence was eroded
And I doubted myself
I would ever touch you again.

Friends come and stare at you in disbelief
Resting quietly in a corner,
Telling themselves most likely
I was merely pretending.

Then the day finally came
When I waved goodbye to you as a gift
Without feeling sad or regretful.
It seemed you had died a natural death
And we now parted as two estranged friends
With nothing else to confide.

How stupid I was
To let you go like that?
Believing you would be gone,
Not knowing instead
You had deeply buried your colors
Inside my emotions
And that your brushes were really my two hands.

The spirit of your art
Had never left its jar of flesh
But waited in silence
Patiently throughout the years
For the first facial sign of Venus
To tear itself away
From the emptiness of its grave
And begin the pathos of resurrection:

Chaos and romance,
Pain and bitterness,
Passion and love.

The Engagement

That what happened
in Las Vegas look
Upon your face
Watching Bikers TV and listening
To riders of a lost cause;
Walking like a ballerina and rebelling
With my art;
A bible of poetry written thousands of years
By wise old men inspired by a God;
Was it something that I said?
A party of chubby girls
Drinking Morgan like a pirate;
The bride groom and bride to be
Opening the floor,
Followed by a calypso of dancers
Switching partners as the music played;
Everyone wearing black and white,
Pretending to be zebras of the night;
The pungent spiciness and flavoured richness

Of a Caribbean fest;

A sudden announcement in the middle of the night

Concerning a wedding to be staged

Somewhere later in a tropical paradise;

Just when things are about to get hot

And temperatures begin to rise

My little daughter signals to us:

'Guys, it's time to leave.'

What if I told You?

What if I told you
That after all these years
I'm still crazy thinking about you?
You'd reply, I honestly
Don't know what to say
And I'd counter with something like this:
Then don't say anything
Cause the last time you were honest
My script didn't go too well
And we had a long Mexican standoff
Which lasted for several months.
Didn't they teach us in school
Honesty isn't always the best policy?
In any event, you and I have walked that road before
And we both knew
We're just two strangers
Sitting on opposite sides of the fence.
I'm not hoping for reciprocity anymore;
I lost that plot a long time ago.

After all, you're only human
And I'm incurably romantic and insane.
I write sleazy poems about sex
And sketch women without their underwear.
No...wait! What if I was wrong?
And I was only listening to my own voice
All the time
Filtering the language of your silence
With words you never said
Miscuing you every time
You wanted to tell me something.
What if I was wrong, indeed?
What if my fantasies are not really fantasies?
What if the artist should wake up one day
And find that his canvas has been replaced
By the people he painted?
What if you were wrong
And I was wrong?
What if the truth never existed at all
And people never had to go to confessions?
I'd serve you coffee in bed with cups of colorful roses,
Take you out in the evenings for a butterfly spin
Across a moonlit sky

To celebrate with you
The birth of a new renaissance of love
And together we would dance
To the Song of Solomon
In the middle of a glowing halo
I would talk to the birds if I have to
Beg them to tweet you the most wonderful melodies
To serenade you in the mornings.
I would if you would and if we both could
But what if we are neither right nor wrong?
And neither is it true nor false?

This is a new poem

Whoever said a poem never ends
Obviously had it wrong
Or either he or she has never written a line.
This is a new poem,
I can tell,
Because the old one died anonymously
Yesterday
Nor has the subject ever been touched.
This time the poet has a name
That alone tells us his life is not a game
His readers may play.
People respond,
Some like it, some don't,
Some dare to criticize it,
Others offer food for thought
But none will ever brush it aside
Or ignore it
The way that pedestrians do passing
An intrusive beggar soliciting on the sidewalks.

My new poem has a purpose and a message
The words I carefully strung together
In the wee hours of the nights and mornings.
It is not some dug up old fashioned sonnet
Rewinding centuries of failed romance
It's about rapping, free styling,
About hip-hop, Def poetry, Spoken Word
Words sung out loud or chanted in the streets,
Stepping in time to the beat,
A mosaic harmony of exotic instruments,
Drum rolling here and there,
Thumping in your face.
You can't miss it or turn away
For when a poem is written
And there's nothing coming back its way,
No sound, murmur or smile
Nothing trivial, greater or more joyful
To supersede its novelty
Then you know it's time
To kill it and begin anew.

You do not talk to me

You do not talk to me,
You do not.
Then again why should you?
To someone who makes pretty women blush
And undress the coldness of their hearts
With just a gentle sweep of his brush;
Nor do you comment
On anything I say,
Nor do you.

Rather than roses
I drew you dozens of portraits
But you preferred his flowers instead;
Rather than diamonds
I wrote you thousands of verses
But to you they were never sparkling enough
Much less to outshine his jewels.
My last poem to you from your lips
Could only suffice a stony silence.

All I ever hungered for
In the desert of your world
Was to stumble and fall upon my delusion,
Watching the melancholy of your face
Slowly disappear above the vaporous horizon,
To unfasten the chains of your sobriety
And navigate the excuses of the past;
To lean across your fence
Like a thief of the night

And pluck the divinity of love
From your heart!

To wear you like a stolen treasure
Around my neck
Even if the fugitive moment more hastily
Should expire than the wink of an eye.

Saying Goodbye to the Rain

Clouds of tissues come floating by
To wipe away the tears from your eyes
Within these prison walls I sigh
Listening to the rain as it silently cries.

Sunlight scampers across the street
Hastily darting out from the porous sky
Among trees birds in black gather to tweet
A requiem for someone preparing to lie.

Brightened by the halo of the sun
Your eyes become a clearer blue;
Obviously the rainbow is a sign we're done
But don't you worry, everything will begin anew.

You taught me how the rain is human,
Sometimes it is happy, sometimes it is sad
A fountain sprinkling with so much fun,
Refreshing as well as nurturing to every lad.

Saying goodbye to the rain
Relieves me of my umbilical cord to the past;
Like you walking away without any pain
Destined to separate the two of us at last

For the Love of Art

Art is love
Art is passion
Art is hatred, anger, jealousy, possession.
The artist is in pursuit of love all the time,
To be inspired,
To do crazy stuff.
Using love as the cycle of his evolution
He becomes transparent
In the eyes of every woman,
Easily predictable but mysterious,
A tyrant in his private fantasies,
Arrogant and strutting like a peacock,
One hand in his pocket,
Head tilted back and upright,
A picture of Napoleon
Crossing the Rubicon.

Reason flees like a coward
As my heart palpitates

To the rhythm of love.
Each word that happily escapes
The secrecy of your lips
Blossoms into a flower,
Transforming my vacuous world
Into a forest of roses.

I watch you navigate
The busy traffic of crowded streets,
Gingerly pedaling all the way
Up to the top of a hill.
Then standing childishly
With outstretched arms
Like a little prophet
You smile forgivingly
At the street below,
Tempted to dance
Because the music
Humming through your earphones
Happens to be a favourite song.

You didn't hear the cries of others
Yelling at you from behind:
Get out of the way, lady!

Have you gone nuts?

Blowing their horns like mad.

Who cares if they're in a hurry?

Life is short.

If you can't stop for a few seconds,

Enjoy that special moment,

One that may never come again,

If you can't let go

Everything that's bothering you,

If you can no longer

Feel the pains of love,

If freedom is not a choice anymore,

If the slope on the other side

Is mired with fears and anxiety

What good is the journey then

That lies ahead of us?

Cups

The man without any cups is orphaned
And stands alone in the garden of Gethsemane;
His sacrifice deferred to another millennium.
Muse-less he winds along
Like a river in search of a bed
An alien inside his head
Accidentally stumbling upon you
With his suitcases of poetry and art
Hoping to become a refugee within your heart
But politely you say no:
He's an artist and must, therefore, create his own cup
For it is the pregnant womb of creation
That cradles our childhood
And delivers us unto the promised utopia of love.
It is the pair of female breasts
Through which the artist is nourished unto manhood
And the nipples he suckles upon for his survival,
Neither empty nor full,
Half empty nor half full
But broken at the moment
And so, cupping his two hands,

The weary traveler tarries on
With his clouds of ashes
Sweeping across the windy seas,
Sprinkling his dust of letters and colors
Into every port and homes of welcoming arms
Until he can rest peacefully his soul
In the cups of his creator's mold.

A Million Minds

Not one, not two,
Nor any other number for that matter
But a million minds away from home;
Across rivers, across oceans, across continents
Sailing with my canvas blowing in the wind;
Navigating my thoughts along highways
That lead to nowhere,
Sometimes by accident
To a land where fairy tales appear to be real,
Breaking the speed limits and sound barriers
As if it's the rule,
Sometimes going through a one way street
Or butting into a no-entry sign;
Flying above deserts and deserted towns
That once prospered in the good old days;
I circle and circle hesitantly,
Scanning the star filled skies
With my piercing eyes
For a heart that remains invisible in time;

A million minds I sail,
A million minds I navigate,
A million minds I fly,
Returning through the curvature of space
To celebrate my galactic failure
With a million poems to extinguish
Before I lay me down to sleep.

Part Three: EROS

"The psychoanalytic liberation of memory explodes the rationality of the repressed individual. As cognition gives way to re-cognition, the forbidden images and impulses of childhood begin to tell the truth that reason denies."

~ Herbert Marcuse

The Seduction

This tale of seduction
Whose ending is neither here nor there
That seems to have no beginning at all,
Like an unfinished masterpiece
Complete in her incompleteness,
Taunting reality with its defiance of death
and immortal pleasure,
Silently and absent-mindedly unattainable,
Wearing the mask of secrecy at a costume ball,
Never content by the ritual of vestal virgins,
Towering in her divinity over masculine worshippers,
An enemy to the bureaucracy of reason and order
Prolonging the agony of failure
By parlaying the reversibility of multiplicity
and repetition:
- Digitizing and cloning of ourselves
- Cancerously overtaking who we are
- Killing our narcissism with excess
In that lethal ah ha moment of suspense

Between the rolling and stopping of a dice,

A seducer in love with the idea of love,

Seducing destiny to survive.

Deal or No Deal?

I have blue eyes, some brown
with a touch of yellow;
My legs are doing fine this fall;
So I thought I'd walk by to say hello
And bare my thighs a little for you to eyeball.

Fucking you in the middle of the street...
Was just a fantasy I think about all the time;
At first, I wanted to do myself again
because you're sweet
But what's the use if all I'm doing is losing my mind?

I'm scared of philosophy
Telling me places are irrelevant
while time is always now
And never teaches anyone not to be;
Hence, badly do I need some answers
to show me how.

Do we have a deal or not?
Or should I do it your way or go my way?

Right now I'm feeling hot

And have nowhere else to stay.

My camera is ready to roll,

Please Doctor Dictator, hurry up and undress
me with your lens,

Spank me as if my butt is cold.

Even though I'm a Goddess, I'm
used to shouting Amens.

And devouring membranes,

Moving among my worshippers rapidly
without mercy,

Leaving behind to tend the remains

My angels who are blood thirsty.

Walking a fine line

Between scandalous and adventurous

To accept a challenge of my kind,

You wonder who else would dare besides
the two of us.

Fuck me! I cried out,

Watching you become speechless and gasping for air

As your tongue struggled to slither
out a word from your mouth

While you stood there before me drooling

and shaking with fear.

I teased you with the gold in my pocket,

Asking when do you want me to come

And cross the Atlantic Ocean to
visit your little hamlet,

Pressing the bell of your door to your bosom.

In anger you tore up our agreement,

Beseeching me to be rough and poetic,

To substitute meteorites for metaphors
and appear more decent,

Making you behave as though you're nothing
but a useless prick.

I immediately blurted out it was swine poetry

But you corrected me, explaining no it was slam

And that I should be screaming, raving,
sweating and acting bitchy;

After all, everyone boasted you
were the best ever ram.

Scorching hot, wet scorching…it made no difference

For what's in a name the lonesome Juliet
queried on her balcony;

I'm a Goddess, I make mountains melt

with my quenchless appetite;

This POTCar button really works like
a mushroom drug on me.

Too Many Etceteras

(an anonymous conversation)

I know what's baffling you:
Did he or did she not?
Aye, such an exquisite work of art!
Maybe it's all in the expression.
You cannot hide.
The true artist can never hide.
I recognize you with your hat on
But you cannot see me
For I am a master of all illusions.
I walk behind many shadows.
And another thing I almost forgot:
You repeat too many etceteras.
A girl has only to hear it once
But two, three times..?
I swear there has to be something more
You're not telling that meets the eye.
And don't you dare give me any more of that
BS artist crap!

About you not being your art.

I've heard that defence a thousand times before.

Or talk to me about detachment

When the alchemy is splashed all over your canvas

Well, is she Puritan or what?

Certainly not French by her accent

Or some other native of that description

Mr. Etcetera!

What do you have to say for yourself now?

I was Worried

I was worried
At what my poems had done to you;
More harm perhaps than one could ever imagine;
Worried that after reading them
For your safety you were forced to flee
To escape my unabated passion,
The voracious incursions
I had inflicted upon my readers;
Engaging you in raw poetic misadventure,
Metaphorical intercourse,
Plundering your wild Amazon forest
Like a Spanish Conquistador
Inexorably in search of the golden El Dorado.
Pleasured by the trail of mighty rivers
And eavesdropping in the vessel of my imagination
I listened to the loud breathing of waterfalls
Emptying the milky cargo of my words
Into a subterranean ocean of your wildest dreams.

I was worried worried!
But then you suddenly re-surfaced
Below the lines of my poems
And told me not to worry,
That you had just returned
From a long summer vacation.

Into the red ocean of your lips

The white ship at sunset
Sails against the tide of loud staccato music,
Voyaging into a deep red ocean
Where it implodes and slowly collapses
Onto a wet welcoming shore.

The wolfish pack leaping out
From the words of a poem
Tears apart the hands of its creator
To exorcize the demons of his imagination
And make cataclysmic love to the world.

My tongue scorching over your lips,
Slides into every volatile part of your body
Lapping away at its flesh
To escape the captivity of my being,
Embracing each other in the joy of darkness.

Such is the collision of two minds wild
With uncontrollable revelry!

The marriage of poet and reader
Consummated on a bed of clouds!
The ultimate resurrection of two soul mates
Dismounted from the crucifix of life
To enter a kingdom of immortal love!

Lust

Too inspired to capture

the intensity of my thoughts,

My eyes are drunk...

My knees are wobbling with excitement...

At any moment I may crumble before your feet....

Inhaling the luscious vegetation

Around me and devouring its pristine leaves.

With open mouth I drink

the cascading juices that flow over me

Meandering like a river into my empty stomach

I ache with unbridled passion...

My hands tremble with desire...

My lips yearn to brush your savoury nipples

Coercing me to reluctantly rise from my dream....

My Epiphanous One

Oh wherefore art thou,
My epiphanous one?
My eyes howl with greediness
Like wolves of the night rearing to snap you up
And mangle every bronze inch of your flesh.

From the kissable toes of your elegant feet
To the ravishing darkness of your liquid hair
The more of you I see
Behind those fortress clothing
The more vivid becomes my vision
And what lies beyond;
The more energized I become
To challenge my destiny.

Your act of nudity
Concretizes my philosophy of love
And the purity of my thoughts,
Liberating me from the dullness of my captivity.

You are erotic as well as intelligent,
You are abstract as well as substance,
You are sex as well as art.

I am fuelled
With the fire of Gods
To pursue a spatial exploration
Of heavenly bodies in the sky,
Uniting my sins with your flesh
Inside the spiritual realm of your temple.
My heart beats for more of you
To transcend my body into your world.

It will take endless orgasms
To create and peel away
The layers of my thoughts
That I may stand un-redacted before you
In the name of love
And kiss every crevice
And every curve on your body;
To baptize myself into your lap
And suck the nectar of your flower
Till I'm intoxicated and quivering
With the ecstasy of madness

And hallucinating to the fragrance

Of your sweet vagina! Ah!

I'm not sexy

So I'm not sexy
To you because I talk a lot
And my words are just full of fluff.
I don't have an Adonis muscle in my body.
I'm only good enough on paper.
You prefer someone who is quiet,
Whose voice is always in the right direction.
I spray all over you
Whenever I open my mouth to speak,
Something you detest but only tolerate
Out of kindness.
But when it seems you've had enough
I get served a restraining order,
Given the cold shoulders
Or seriously warned to shut the fuck up
Or else.
And even though we spend a lot of time together
Your mind is somewhere else
And you cannot stop to drool about him:

How sexy his voice rings in your ears
Though he never utters a word
Which pisses me off by the way
For no reason at all
Yet somehow I like the anger it provokes
Cause now I can write another poem
To tell you how I feel.
I don't care if it's real or not
And I know you think it's fun
To burst my bubble every time
Or toss my ego through the window
But hey..I don't go around pretending
I'm superior or playing someone's hero.
I wear skinny jeans and a cap
And I don't carry any tattoos on my skin
Or piercings in my ears.
My game is simple:
I talk, you talk, I'm inspired, I write
Sometimes we do a little Cha Cha Cha
If we have to
But never silent
Cause everyone knows I'm not sexy
And I don't dance to any music except the salsa.

Veggie Monologue

V is for the veggie on top

Eat as much as you like

Guys love to come at my restaurant

Girls, too, sometimes when they are lonely

I do not know of any other meal so pleasurable

Eyes tend to run wild at the sight of my apple pie.

Many men masticate over their plates

Others simply lick the platter bone
dry with their tongues

No one has ever complained about my menu

Or the natural juices I pour

Like a river flowing out of the Amazon forest

Oh Gawd! is a phrase I often hear repeatedly

Gyrating and hitting that high note

Unaware that the neighbours might
be listening to them

Entering noisily through the front door

The Vaginal Hammer

Can you hear it?
A voice drifting over the waves,
Blowing across miles of oceans
Like a refugee fleeing from his soul,

An anonymous poem
Written by a young office assistant
Left unnoticeably lying in the dip
Of a beguiling middle aged secretary,

Shakespeare rubbing his chin,
Pondering the fate of a noble character,
Hesitating at the crucial moment
Whether or not the time to act is now,

Nervously opening a sealed envelope
To end the unbearable silence
Of an eagerly awaited response,
Fatigued by all the anticipated suspense,

The bramble bush burning
At the top of a holy mountain
Revealing secrets from a divine origin
To a prophet lost in the wilderness,

A stripper curling around
And hugging the iciness of a silvery pole,
Selectively peeling away each item of apparel
Before tossing at you her vaginal hammer,

That split twenty six seconds
When all you need to do is to pull the trigger
And watch love glide hopefully and safely
Into your victim's heart.

Part Four: Acts of Defiance

"My consciousness is not illuminated with ultimate radiances. Nevertheless, in complete composure, I think it would be good if certain things were said. These things I am going to say, not shout. For it is a long time since shouting has gone out of my life. So very long. . . ."

~ Franz Fanon

Superficiality

The way they often hide

Behind the transparency of their lies

Makes you want to throw up.

That institutional fabric validating
every wrongful act,

Turning everything around to extract the meaning

From what is said and done,

Making enemies of the poor and innocent

Fleeing for their lives,

Using whatever motives to sanctify
their crimes against humanity

Staring at you and pointing their fingers!

Poverty is expensive but not if you're rich.

I've pitched myself down to the bottom to ask,

Is it time yet?

And how much more void can the universe become?

Ironically shooting myself with a
big bang at the beginning

To die even before I was born

As if to contradict the theory of physics

With my metaphorical appearance.

A civilisation of misogynists under siege

Terrorized by the promiscuity of the vagina,

Burning witches at stakes,

Enforcing chastity with the crack of an iron whip

Gagging a woman's mouth

While concealing the devilish curves on her body

How vain was Adam to let Eve think

She could ever tempt him with the
mere bite of an apple?

Smile because you're unhappy,

Run like it's the last day in your life,

Welcome the misfortunes and horrors of war.

After all, democracy is but a multiple choice,

Two extremities of the same coin

And whoever is lucky to win the toss

Dances to the tune of the invisible hand.

The profanity of child sacrifices necessitated
to impress the Gods

For whom art once postured as the
last bastion of freedom

Now becomes the ultimate art of artifice

Sadly more real than the humanity of its subjects.

The media brags about it everyday in the news.

No one has time to raise a finger any more.

Nor is it a question of whether I dare or dare not.

For it is either I sink or swim

Or go with the flow like all the rest of us.

Utopia of parallel Worlds

Each time I make an overture

To meet you half way

You push me away,

Triumphantly in your armoured defence.

You, on the bitter right

And I, struggling on the left,

Internalizing the utopia of my parallel worlds

To unite us hopefully across the political divide,

But no peace dividend could ever compensate

The advantage you maintain,

Not even the continued illegal occupation
and settlement

Of lands belonging to another.

For time is on your side, you secretly reaffirm,

Constantly reading to me the riot act:

One step forward, two steps back!

My invective appeal to reason

Solidifies your recalcitrance

To any alternative but a hard Brexit.

Those immigrants must leave, I hear you insist,

And take their religion of hate with them

Back to hell where they belong.

After all, what did the British ever
do to any foreigner?

In Iraq, Libya, Afghanistan and Syria

We fought to liberate those savages

From brutal dictators habitually gassing
their own people

And how do they pay us back?

By launching assaults on our peaceful
law abiding citizens,

Taking away our council houses from us

For which we have been waiting many years.

The EU is to be castigated for our failing
infrastructure,

De-funding our National Health System,

Reducing our wages and benefits,

Unleashing rampant unemployment

In our cities and our towns,

Privatizing the public transportation system

And every other public service to enrich
the one percent.

Our real leaders are the faceless bureaucrats
hiding in Brussels,

Dictating to us when we must leave

As if we are the victims trapped inside
a hotel in California.

I don't have a moustache or a beard,

Things that you obviously idolize

Which perhaps remind you of the glorious 60's,

The days when boomers were called radicals

Fatigued in bohemian outfits

With long hair flowing over their shoulders

And messianic beards covering their chins,

Protesting against wars and chanting

"Give Peace a Chance!"

Me, I am sadly more conservative in appearance

But still carrying the rebellious
mind of my younger years

While you, on the other hand, remain
stubbornly close

And more conservative to the Golden
Age of Empire building.

#Why Tulsi

Critics may call this a love poem,

Denying your Goddess-like beauty,

The signature Mallen hair streak that rocked viewers

On that memorable first night,

Conspicuously famous in history for
going against the grain.

Two hundred years ago you might've easily
been crowned

The Warrior Princess of the West

But even so the naysayers are more afraid
of your hawkish love for peace,

Your honesty and purity of heart,

The compassion and humility ebbing through
the measured pace of your lips,

The wisdom of your emotion,

So calm and yet so open,

Ready to meet your adversaries across
the political spectrum

To welcome them with the open spirit of Aloha

Anyone who pushes back

Against the smear of the mainstream media

Deemed a fanatic, extremist or cult follower

Who is blinded by the warmth of
your nurturing voice,

An Assad apologist, Russian bot, unpatriotic,

Homophobic, Hindu nationalist, anti-Islamic,

Defender of torture and targeted use of drones

To serve and protect the people of America,

Attacked from all sides, left, right and centre,

None of them listening to what you say in interviews
and town halls.

Time and again news anchors repeating
the same questions over and over,

Brazenly attempting to bully you in public
and put words into your mouth,

Some of them so scripted and having no clue

What it means to be called a toady.

You made it known to us at the beginning

You were entering this race as an underdog,

Someone with whom many of the grassroots
can empathize

And even though your numbers far exceed

the donor threshold

The polls are fixed to keep you out from going further,

Especially after that savage TKO to
one of their favourites

And before that, knee capping one
of their warmongers.

I've seen a few of your supporters fell before
the fake narrative,

Become despondent by the negative
news of rigged polls,

I've seen young progressives

blend themselves in with the mainstream,

Anchoring their analyses on manufactured truths,

I've heard comments like, "She's out,

Oh she's just a fringe candidate, a
one issue candidate."

Little do they care or stop to reflect

On the trillions of dollars wasted
on regime removal wars,

Dollars that could easily help to
pay for Medicare for All,

The writing off of student debts,

Create decent liveable wage paying jobs,

The transitioning to a greener safer environment

And yes, an end to untold human

suffering and global instability

That would defuse the refugee crises in
Europe, Africa and Latin America,

Remove the need for expensive border walls,

Scapegoating of immigrants and the ramping up

of White Supremacy,

Making people over profits the centre of
the nation's economic prosperity!

The stoics of ancient Greek philosophy will ask,

What does it matter if in the end

the playbook is always the same?

I'm almost laughing at the top of my head

To witness how some of us are so quick to fall in line

And you wonder how they beat us,

How they beat us at Brexit?

How they whipped our asses in 2016?

The best opportunity ever is before us now

To make the biggest change in our lives.

In Tulsi we have a leader and woman for all season

Why fritter away our chances for vague platitudes,

For wolf kings and Queens who will misguide you

With slogans that any Blue will do?

At the Door of Conscience

The posse of cardboard men
All dressed in dark blue uniforms
Knocks at every door of conscience.
They come to arrest my decadent words
Dripping like semen over papered vaginas
From the gaping mouths of hookers
Whose legs are widely spread over a writer's desk.

Beneath the tapestry of underwear
I hear biblically inspired hymns
In a battle to purge the souls of young
women and children
Disentangled from their emotions,
Screaming in horror
At the flashing voices of liberty
Igniting a purple sky.

The notoriety of mandatory drafts
Summon young men to arm and salute their penises.
No one is safe anymore

To escape the pain of emasculation.

In the game of politicking and compromises
The stakes are high and gamblers are untouchables
Lives are measured not by coffee spoons
But through the barrel of loaded rifles.

The more he evolves
Into a predatory beast of tomorrow,
Lording himself over the flies,
Symptomatic of a cancerous society
Pillaging its own intestines,
Celebrating the obscene dichotomy of rich and poor,
The more we blindly subjugate ourselves
To omnipotent rulers of the land.

The Referendum

The poll driven plebs
Roar excitedly
As word reaches them:
The leaves have just jumped ahead
With a six point lead
And only four more days to go.
Genuine panic escalates among the remains
Unlike the trumped up rumours
of their paranoid foes.
World leaders, international organizations,
The best of brilliant minds, eminent scientists
All are baffled and in awe at what they're witnessing:
The confiscation of man's finest possession.
The gift of reason superseded by
the magic wand of faith
And judgement rhetorically unfounded.
Elsewhere signs of another holocaust
Looming ominously in the near horizon
As another lunatic takes the centre stage

Massively cheered on by another furious rabble.

Xenophobia is couched in the sacred
language of sovereignty

Justified by crimes against migrants

and Malthusian fears of over-population.

The masses are visually impaired and overloaded

By what they see and hear in the media.

Leavers have no time for inquiries,

Verification or weighing of the pros and cons.

Everything is fixed and only a matter of days remain

Before the early autumn arrives.

Facts are vaporized into smokescreens

Hiding a resounding "No!"

The old Roman trick is again at work

To divert and ventilate the frustrations

Of a riotous mob,

Politicians leverage to win either way

At the expense of their constituencies,

Exploiting the existential choice

To leave or not to leave

Where the only defence is the ending,

I remain yours truly forever...

The Election

Thank God it's over
And you won!
Just as we had hoped.
At the beginning we were worried
that it seemed so close.
And when he jumped ahead of you
We sighed heavily, thinking
It was over for you
And for us,
For the rest of the world
Who were rooting for you.
I almost vomited
Feeling the nausea building up
Inside me.
Michael Moore's good Samaritan gesture,
The baritone voice of Neil Diamond on the phone
Appeared to be all in vain.
You could see the joy and rapture
In the wide opened eyes of the other side

'I only prepared a winning speech,'
He told the anxious media
As though destiny had crowned him
To be ordained the new emperor
While the rest of the world trembled
Feeling the vibrations of an oncoming earthquake,
Fearing the worst,
A sign of the prophetic Armageddon,
Shouts of apartheid and death to the infidels,
No mercy for the poor and helpless,
A world ravaged by the chaos of wars,
And a Masonic belief in the right of might.
Then the numbers magically reversed
As though David Copperfield had intervened
And we saw for the first time
You had taken the lead,
Jumping ahead as far as you can
Like a kangaroo chased by sadistic poachers.
All of a sudden in a matter of minutes
It was over.
Florida went down like a giant tree
Collapsing to the ground
We all stood up from our seats

Shocked and in disbelief
At what had happened.
All around there were cries of jubilation
'You did it! You did it!' they clamoured.

The day I stopped to smile

I never thought this day would come:
A self fulfilling prophesy to some
When he would win the electoral college
Pushing his opponent over the edge.
At the beginning when we saw the
first results come in
No one bothered for we knew she would win
But after a while his numbers began to grow
While hers hardly seemed to flow
Apparently stuck behind his infamous wall
Where nothing moved at all.
This was not happening, my inner
voice cried out to me
How could this be?
Did the polls get it wrong again?

A Wind of Change

A wind of change
Goose stepping across the oceans
You can feel it coming
Threatening the status quo
Accompanied by watery drums thumping
Against the crystalline shores

No more roadblocks, please
I've had enough of your tease
It's not as if I were an escapist Houdini
Defying the laws of attraction
How often can a man retreat
Only to be shackled by his hopes again

The savage roar of a lunatic fringe
Hailing horrors of another holocaust
From the barrel of their bitter hatred
Rattling accusations like bullets
Where bodies of innocent women and children

Lay splattered on the reddened grass
Conversations are short
The hours spin away into blackness
There's no time for exhortation
Soon enough major decisions have to be made
The day is already done and I'm off to bed
So good night to you my dearest friend

Those Pictures

Those pictures,
Those blue and star spotted faces,
Whose virginal future had just been raped
By senile baby boomers
Dishonouring the memory of Woodstock,
No longer able to recognize
The flowered revolution of love and hope
And the difference between change and anarchy,
Rebelling now against the movement of time,
Terrified by others who are different,
Exclusively retreating into the glory of their own egos
A motherland that once conquered half the world,
Now intolerant of strangers coming to its shores,
Separating us from them
With delusions of fanned fear by extremists
Ready to amplify our insecurity,
Taking away our jobs, our homes, all of our benefits,
Those youthful sad faces,
Those pictures,

Those heavenly stars,

The blueness of lost horizons

And avatar images

Telling tales of more than a thousand words old,

Chanting, "We love EU"

In the choir of voices

Distinctly drifting and migrating freely
across borders and oceans,

Oh the guilt, the selfishness and irresponsibility

Into which we had tunnelled ourselves,

Reluctantly afraid to step aside

And re-open our hearts!

Whose Voice?

Whose voice it is you listen to?
When the wind howls at you
From the distant shores of nowhere
Across the Indian Ocean,
Across the Pacific,
Across the Atlantic Ocean;
When the phone rings clamorously at nights
And no one answers at the other end.

Whose voice I hear
Murmuring within the deep dungeons of my head
Synchronizing with every stroke of a clock's hands
Is it really true that I care?

When the mighty tears roll out from a faded blue sky
And no one, not even the friend you trusted,
Comes running over to your rescue
Armed with soothing words to
mop away a single drop.

Whose voice is it?

Whose voice is it?

That cries out from the hollowness of the dark

Echoing a name you wouldn't dare to recall;

A voice choking and drowning in
a sea of unforgiveness.

Whose voice is it you hear

Muted by the ears of silence,

Screaming without pain,

Laughing without happiness;

Whose voice it is

Singing alone the unsung lyrics of a ghostly requiem

Whose voice is the deep sigh that awakens you?

If not the wailing of mothers

At funerals, at weddings and even at birthdays;

Whose voice is the graffiti of the streets

Resisting the violence and abuse against women,

The little children without parents,

The hungry and the disabled;

Whose voice do we dance to?

When the music no longer plays

When the clapping ceases

And all you can hear

Is only the sound of your thoughts

Curling up inside you like an unborn child.

Waiting for Something

I have found
Tears in laughter,
Loneliness in friendship,
Hate in love,
Greed in satisfaction,
War in peace,
Despair in hope.
The futility of long hours
Waiting for something,
For someone,
Impossible,
Inevitable,
Spontaneously recurring,
A human race
Mutating against itself,
Inversely portrayed
In a celluloid mirror,
A concave world
Shamefully disembowelled

Carrying within it
We the ostracized lovers
Like a virus of unfulfilled dreams
Inoculated at every opportunity
To avoid the sharing of our sweetness
While we watch
In woeful silence
Those that do
And disastrously fail.

Reversing to be hit by a Truck

Reversing to be hit by a truck
Is where we're stuck,
Worrying about issues that never budge.
Who are we to judge?
When we've all been to Sunday schools
And none of us are any fools.

Jesus Christ died on a cross,
Regretting he might've fought for the wrong cause.
So let's hold on to the essence of the moment
Ere it's too late and we're forced to suffer in torment.

You say the world has too much freedom;
That people complain but have no symptom;
That it's just their voices they're anxious to hear.
No one cares about the rights you share;
The bitter undertones you try to hide
Or whether or not you ever lied.

Aiming your pistol at me

To demonstrate anger is the key
If changes we desire should ever come about.
Shall I take to the streets and shout?
Join the mob to make a point?
Or be afraid lest I disappoint?

A bird on a window sill
Courage in me seems to instill
As I rise to the song of its call
And begin a poem that hopefully
will appeal to all!

Rebel! Rebel!

Rebellion! Rebellion!
Is all I hear
People shouting without any fear.
But who is to blame?
They that have no shame.
How can anyone be defiant
When all around us is a tyrant
Surveilling us with his cameras
Even in the bedroom with only our pajamas.
They listen to every word we say
And never fail to record us every day.
How can we rebel
When we have nothing more to tell?
They make us think we're free
But fool us with everything we see.
Rebel! Rebel!
Why should I
If either way I'm going to die?
Others better than me have tried

Which has only made me cried

Life ebbs on

The soldiers are gone

Replaced by machines that have no feeling

At the noise of women and children screaming

Need I say more?

Many a times in the past I swore

But today my voice is worn

And like an old man I am torn

Rebel if you must

Just leave me alone to rust

I have no quarrel with anyone

All I want is to have a little bit of fun

Before I close my eyes

And bid this world my final goodbyes.

Breaking all the Rules

Breaking all the rules they said
Will never get you anywhere you want to go; instead
You'll end up roaming the streets
Alone out there   just like all those crazy creeps
Who end up pushing   a Georgie bundle trolley
And smelling and looking dirty in their folly!

People will laugh at you and point their fingers,
Telling their little ones you must've
been an intractable sinner
Who throughout your life never believed in Him
Until one day the lights in it   all
of a sudden grew dim.

But they were wrong
And I knew it all along
Rules are made by schools
And education is just another set of tools
Aimed at disciplining the minds of poor little boys
To turn them into robotic toys

I didn't want to be a stereotype

So I left without becoming a prototype

If there're any rules a woman should follow

It's this: She should never let herself
become a shadow

Let the men know   you'll never agree

And that you'll always fight   to remain forever free

So listen up to me carefully I say

I don't need any of your rules to make me stay

Or keep me locked away inside

As if I have nothing to show or hide

I will push the boundaries as far as they go

I don't care if you tell me no

You may berate me all you like   about your respect

And threaten me to disconnect

But I'm a survivor

So nothing you say or do

Will ever shame me into becoming   a quitter.

Outrage

For many of us
Who support you
This is an emotional time
And so I am impelled
To express my outrage.
We're tired of fighting the good fight
And being the loser every time
Though we knew we would not be surprised.
Still the disappointment is hurting
Not to see you again in action
Taking out another establishment crony
In the dog and pony show.
Like the grim reaper
You're so feared by the fixers
Holding on to their last hope
A feeble old granny way past her time
But whose speed the mainstream boasts
Is faster than her surging in the polls

Summing Up

Summing up
what we've done so far in this round:
First we vacillated
Over love and attachment
With several cups of freshly brewed tea
Until I could bear it no longer
And gingerly tap danced my way to the washroom
Where I was feeling so depressed
I wanted to hide behind my shadow
But just as I hit rock bottom
And slowly began my ascent
From the depths of my poverty
You boasted about your musicians
And brandished before my tearful eyes
Two pieces of jewels which you proudly announced
Gave you la douleur exquise
How you swore you had no need
For any bruck packit man
Who'll only ruin your promising life

So what's a poet to do?

Except to voice his anger

And rebel against his cruel fate?

Acknowledgement

I am deeply indebted to the POTCar Circle for the infectious atmosphere and irresistible challenge that kept me motivated to go after my poetic aspirations. Many of the poems in this collection have formed part of my contribution to the diverse repertoire of excellent Caribbean poetry written by the group. In this regard I am especially grateful to Ric Couchman, whom we all unanimously looked up to as the Dean of the group and who was very instrumental in introducing me as a newcomer to many of my other fellow Caribbean writers. Special thanks cannot be forgotten to Cynthia Pearson as Chairwoman of the Circle whose exemplary leadership kept us busy and united in our artistic awakening. Others such as the brilliantly talented Diane Allen West, Austin George Henry, David Pearson (alias The Rock), Leighton Spalding and Veneisha Rochester and my own close friend from childhood, Steve Persuad, have all had a knock on effect on me as a young amateur poet philosophically overflowing with post modernist ideas.

Likewise, I am also fortunate to have made the acquaintances of many beautiful friends on social media who provided me with lots of material and reasons to translate our shared experience and enjoyment into the appropriate literary format. I hesitate to single out any of them of them in particular but they know who they are and while some of them have moved on to the greener pastures and have found much more enterprising new colleagues without bothering to look back I am no less obliged to each of them for the profound way in which they have all awoken my inner artistic demon.

Last but not least, my family has been extremely patient and tolerant of my frequent lengthy introspective disengagement from the real world to indulge in my artistic passions. To them I owe you the entire world and could never stop beseeching your forgiveness.

About The Author

Samuel Mann

Samuel Mann is a self styled existen-
tialist and post modernist artist
seeking to explore innovative ways
of presenting poetry as a packaged
performance and audio visual art.
He is one of three co-authors of a book on Art and the
Creative Process.

Praise For Author

"Pushing the boundaries with his creative imaginings Mann allows his speakers to loosen their tongues and hearts to say what each aging man is dying to say and feel but has shown restraint. In his almost blasphemous thinking and questionings, Mann's poetry explodes on the pages, inviting even the young to become curious about life and what it means to age freely, to fall in love, laugh, to break the rules and experience the joy of living."
~Cynthia Pearson, Chair of POTCar (Poets of the Caribbean) Circle

"The narratives revel in the constancy of rebirth and the raging against time. The writer lives through the eyes of the anguished rebel facing the firing squad of reality, fully sober to life's eventualities. Transitioning towards higher increments of wisdom, the writer avoids the Sartrean ideal of an existence seeped in nothingness, but arrives nonetheless, at that place in which he embraces its crushing finality."
~Dianne Allen West, Editor

www.ingramcontent.com/pod-product-compliance
Lightning Source LLC
Chambersburg PA
CBHW070805050426
42452CB00011B/1901